WHEN THE BALL GOES FLAT

*The Athlete's Guide to Rise Up
and Pursue Their Purpose After Sports*

MICHAEL BARHAM

Copyright © 2021
Michael Barham
WHEN THE BALL GOES FLAT
The Athlete's Guide to Rise Up
and Pursue Their Purpose After Sports
All rights reserved.

No part of this publication may be reproduced, distributed, or transmitted in any form or by any means, including photocopying, recording, or other electronic or mechanical methods, without the prior written permission of the publisher, except in the case of brief quotations embodied in critical reviews and certain other non-commercial uses permitted by copyright law.

Michael Barham

Printed in the United States of America
First Printing 2021
First Edition 2021

ISBN: 978-0-578-88873-6

10 9 8 7 6 5 4 3 2 1

Because of the dynamic nature of the internet, any web addresses or links contained in this book may have changed since publication and may no longer be valid. The views expressed in this work are solely those of the author and do not necessarily reflect the views of the publisher, and the publisher disclaims any responsibility for them.

Library of Congress Control Number: 2021907814

WHEN THE BALL GOES FLAT

Table of Contents

Dedication 1
Introduction 5
Chapter 1 9
   No More Air
Chapter 2 13
   Responsibility
Chapter 3 17
   Self-Evaluation
Chapter 4 23
   Shift Your Mind
Chapter 5 27
   Shift Your Habits
Chapter 6 33
   Shift Your Environment
Chapter 7 41
   Find The Gap
Chapter 8 47
   What's Your Superpower?
Chapter 9 53
   Knowing Is Not Enough
Chapter 10 57
   T.A.M.E. Your Goals
Chapter 11 61
   The Power of Serving
Chapter 12 67
   Patiently Aggressive
Epilogue 73
About the Author 75

Dedication

Special word of thanks to my wife, Kaitlyn Barham. You've been here with me every step of the way. Thank you for being my number 1 supporter throughout my process of growth. You are the main reason that this project finally is complete. There are no words that I can express to show my gratitude to you. I love you more than anything in the world.

Special word of thanks to my children, Khloe & Kylie Barham. I do my best to provide you with all the love and support that you deserve. My favorite words to hear are, "I love you dad." My hope is that my impact on your "life" is larger than my impact on the world. I love you both, and I'm proud to be your dad.

Special word of thanks to my mother, Valencia Barham. I am grateful beyond measure that you decided to have me even with all that you were facing. You instilled so much inside me just by watching the fighter you are. Thanks for all the love and support that you have shown me over the years. I pray that the work that I do makes you proud to call me your son.

Special word of thanks to my uncle, Herman Barham III. Your selfless act of raising me while being a college student means the world to me. You introduced me to the game of basketball and coached me into a great player. The seed that you planted inside me will bloom across the world as athletes' lives are transformed. Your journey as an entrepreneur was the passion behind me becoming an entrepreneur and producing other entrepreneurs during this process. I love you and thank you for it all!

Special word of thanks to my grandparents, Barbara Mcghee, Earnest Mcghee, Herman Barham II, Annie Barham, Inez Carter, and the late Frank Carter. You all played a huge part in the village that raised me. Every prayer, word of encouragement, or lesson that you taught me was vital to my growth process.

Special word of thanks to my brother, James Poindexter. Wow, thank you for opening the door for me to start coaching at the high school level in 2012. You taking me in allowed me to gain the experience that I needed to go to the next level in my life. You preached to our players every day to give their all because sooner or later, the ball was going flat.

Special word of thanks to my friends, Martez and Genesis Nalls. First, you have been very supportive friends from day one to my family and me. You both have been a huge part of growing my vision to the place where it is today. Thank you for every photo and video shoot that you've captured for me that has helped me stand out from the pack. Your work will continue to be featured all over the world as my impact increases.

Special word of thanks to my pops, Orion Carter. Thanks for the words of encouragement and support that you provide. The revitalization process has been a great journey for me. I am excited to see how our past will be the healing for others' futures.

Special word of thanks to Pastor Camilo and first lady Sheila Fuller. Thank you for helping me build a great spiritual foundation during some of the toughest years of my life. Your love for impacting the lives of young people is inspiring and contagious. You showed me what it looks like firsthand to sacrifice for a mission and be the change you want to see.

Special word of thanks to friend Kerry Turner. Thank you for being such a pivotal part of my transition after sports. You were more like a big brother than a best friend. You taught me how to change my oil, change my tire, and so much more. I'm positive that you would be a part of this journey of chasing purpose if you were still alive. I promise to fill the same gap for young men that you filled for me with your wisdom and support.

When The Ball Goes Flat 6 Week Boot Camp

Sign up today at
www.michaelbarhamelevates.com

Introduction

Welcome and thank you for purchasing *When The Ball Goes Flat*. I hope this book will empower you through your transition after sports and activate you to start pursuing your purpose with your gifts.

If you are reading this book, you are trying to figure out what to do with your life after sports has ended. You know there is more to your life, but you don't know where to start.

I know that you are struggling with the pain of how sports ended. You really don't understand the value that you have to add to the world because the only thing on which you have focused was being the best athlete possible. Ball was "life." Now, you don't have a clue about how to live life without the ball.

Listen, you were made on purpose for a purpose. You have a gift inside you that will impact the entire world. You can become confident in yourself the same way you were confident in the athlete in you. You can overcome your pain by taking responsibility for your growth. You also can find your purpose by finding needs and healing hurts.

They call me "Mr. Cap Less and Grind More." I am known as the "Transition Coach" for athletes after sports. I've coached high school basketball and have been a business owner for over 10 years. Over time, I've helped hundreds of athletes transition from sports and walk in their purpose.

I remember when the ball went flat for me. I was hurt and angry, and I blamed anything and anyone for my failures in life. I was depressed because I felt purposeless and had no clue what to do with my life next. My desire to get clout caused me to make some uncharacteristic decisions. A drug transaction that went wrong quickly showed me that the street life my friends were living was not for me.

After attending 4 of my friends funerals in one year and seeing my face in their obituaries, I knew it was a sign that I needed to change my life, and I needed to do it fast. Eventually, I took responsibility for my growth and started using my gifts to walk in my purpose.

Since then, I've coached high school basketball, became a bestselling author, started a profitable business, secured contracts to train teachers and students, and helped hundreds of athletes transition after sports.

The purpose of this book is to give athletes a process to start building themselves up and equip them with tangible strategies to find their gifts and pursue their purpose. I've taken strategies that I teach my clients and put them in this book.

The content of this book will not work on it's own. The strategies in this book only will work if you read each page and chapter and implement what you learn. If you skip chapters, stop reading, or decide to put it of, then these strategies won't work. I want you to take these strategies and put them into immediate action.

Stop being stuck in your transition after sports. Your purpose is waiting for you to come get it. Once you read *When The Ball Goes Flat*, you will be equipped fully to elevate your life and become more than an athlete.

Michael Barham

Follow me on Social Media

Facebook: Michael Barham Elevates
Instagram: @Michael Barham_Elevates
TikTok: @MichaelBarhamElevates
LinkedIn: Michael Barham Elevates
Twitter: @Michael Barham Elevates
Clubhouse: Michael Barham

Chapter 1
No More Air

Ten, *nine, eight, seven, six, five...* it's starting to get real to me. My heart is beating like an HBCU band as I fight to hold back the tears. I am looking at my teammates on the sideline because it's about to be over. My entire senior year flashed before my eyes as the clock ran out.

Now, I'm not just hurt about losing the game. I'm hurt because reality is setting in that this was my last game. After fighting through the adversity of going through three coaches, I'm filled with hurt, anger, frustration, disappointment. I'm filled with all these things as that clock hit zero because the reality has hit me that the ball finally has gone flat.

I know what you're feeling. It's rough. You just wish you had one more time, one more second, one more shot, one more snap, or one more swing. You're remembering all those things your coach told you: *Don't cheat yourself. Play every game like it's your last. Don't be selfish. Play for more than just yourself.* You're thinking to yourself, *There are no college offers. There are no letters. There's nothing.*

You bought into this concept that ball is life, so you literally have spent every single second working on the game, thinking about the game, and being the game. Now, the game you put your heart in has ended. First, I want to let you know that you are not alone, and I know at this moment, you feel like you're alone because it's only you. However, more than seven million athletes don't play college sports after high school. In 2021, the global pandemic increased those numbers due to the college level expanding another year of eligibility to the athletes who already were in college.

While everyone is talking about D1 or bust or D2, D3, or JUCO options, you're thinking about what is left for you to do. You have no clue of what to do next because now reality has set in. This is it for sports. It's frustrating after you're done. The crowd is gone, and there is no one else cheering you on. There's no one else who is talking about you. You're not the center of attention anymore.

It doesn't seem like people or things value you the way they did when you had that ball in your hand. You've shifted into a different category. You now are considered just a "regular" person, and that terrifies you. I'm not minimizing what you're going through right now because I felt that pain, and I understand it. However, now, it's time for you to build yourself.

Most athletes only focus on building the athlete and not the person. They practice all their moves and everything else they've been told to practice, but they never intentionally build up themselves. Don't believe the lie that all of your best days are behind you when all the plays and memories are going through your head. Don't believe the lie that there is no value left inside you to add to anything or anyone in the world. You still can make the rest of your life the best of your life. It's going to take you being very intentional and committed to the process of your growth.

Now, I'm not telling you that this transition is going to be easy because it is not. You just need it to be possible more than you need it to be easy. It will be filled with adverse moments, but you've been built to handle adversity because you saw it daily while you played the game that you love.

I went through a very dark time when I finished playing sports. I was full of bitterness and anger. I was depressed and felt purposeless. The things that I did to pursue my purpose after sports will be very helpful for you on your journey to find what's next for you.

Reflection

Have you focused on building yourself as a person more than you have as an athlete?

Are you willing to commit to developing to the best version of yourself?

Chapter 2

Responsibility

Winston Churchill said, "The price of greatness is responsibility." Now, I did want greatness, but the last thing that I wanted to do was accept responsibility for anything at all. I was angry and couldn't see my part in anything that I'd done that got me to this point. I had a tough senior year. It was my pandemic before the COVID-19 pandemic. You see, I was a late bloomer. I didn't start games until my 12th grade year. The pressure of it being my last year of high school caused me to lock in and do the work that I needed to stand out and get a starting position. I had no clue that my world was about to be shaken up, and we were going to go through a couple of coaches.

It was a regular afternoon. Well, it seemed like a regular afternoon. My teammates and I were in the gym shooting around right before practice. Coach was a little late, but we didn't think anything of it. Moments later, the principal came into the gym and called us all to the library. As we were walking, we were talking to each other and asking, "What could it be?" We had no clue of the earthquake that was about to shake our lives when we got there.

There was a look of nervousness on the principal's face to match our feelings, so you could tell that something was really, really wrong. We felt like something bad was about to happen. It almost was like that look on your parents' face when you know that you took something extra from the pantry, and you weren't supposed to do that, or you had that bad report card and had to make that walk of shame home. You knew you were about to get in deep, deep trouble. That was the look that the principal had on his face when we walked inside the library.

We were not really given an explanation, but we were now told that our coach was let go, and we would have a new coach. Immediately, the room got silent, but you definitely could hear snot and tears rolling down my other teammates' faces. Although it did hurt very badly, we mustered up the strength to come together and move forward and accept the new coach and what he was pushing us to do. We met at 5:00 a.m. and participated in two-a-day practices. We did what it took to make a run because we had a special team.

Then, we showed up for one 5:00 a.m. practice, but there was no coach. Days went by, and eventually it made the news. There was a missing persons report, and later the authorities found him, but he never came back to coach us. Now, as teenagers, we had no clue of what happened, but there was a lot of speculation among the team members. After that fiasco, we were now on coach number 3 as they moved the B team coach up to lead us.

We were motivated enough to stick together and fight our way through the playoffs. We made it to the Elite Eight, but that was not enough for the championship or to get us the looks we wanted for scholarships. I couldn't wait to blame having three coaches in one year for my inability to make it to the next level. I completely excluded the work that I didn't put in or the times that I was enjoying myself on social media instead of being focused on getting better. I completely excluded the time that I spent chasing down girls when I could have been getting better with my teammates who were in the gym religiously. They were the ones who actually got scholarships.

I excluded it all because I was only interested in pointing a finger and finding something or someone to blame. I was facing the fact that I was about to become an adult, and I also was dealing with the fact that my father had just reached out to me for the first time in six years. I was so focused on blaming him for the growth that I could have had. I thought, *If I had a dad growing up, I would have a scholarship.* I was so caught up on blaming him for the things that I felt like I should have known about becoming a man.

Here I was. I was going into life, and I did not know how to be a man, and I was terrified. I was focused on the blame game so much that I discounted the lessons I learned from the men who I did experience growing up. I was looking around and waiting to point the finger towards somebody because my only option was community college. At that point, I didn't take my grades seriously. Additionally, I had not taken the ACT. My assumption was that the test was only for the individuals who had scholarships already or had the grades to receive one.

I want you to know that the blame game leaves you the same. I blamed everyone else for my failures, and the results stayed the same until I took responsibility for myself.

One of the things I want you to do is take responsibility for your growth because the life that you want to live, or the life that's ahead of you only will be different if you do something different.

Now, I get it. You may have had a rough upbringing like me, and we can go tit for tat about the things that didn't go our way. However, I do want you to understand that in order for you to be the person who you want to be and reach the greatness that you want to reach, from here on out, you have to be in control of yourself, and you have to take full responsibility for your life.

I get it, this is the last thing you want to do in your mind. You still may be hurt by some deep stuff, and you feel that you are letting whoever hurt you of the hook by taking responsibility for your growth. My focus is on getting you better and centering your focus off of him or her. That person is living his or her best life while you still remain stuck pointing the fingers.

One of the ways to shift your thinking is to control what you can control. You can't control how sports ended, but you can control the life that you build from here. Am I saying the space that you're in is not somebody else's fault? Am I saying that no one did anything to you? No. I'm telling you that if it's always somebody else's fault, you never will have a different outcome or the control of your outcome. Make a choice right now. Will you commit to taking full responsibility for your growth from this day forward?

Chapter 3
Self-Evaluation

John Wooden said "without proper self-evaluation, failure is inevitable." Listen, I was failing, and self-evaluation wasn't even close on my list of things I thought that I should do to fix it. I was a pretty normal guy who didn't get in a lot of trouble, but the things my friends were doing were very tempting.

Hear me out when I tell you that you were not made to fit in so don't try. I understand right now, there's going to be pressure in life to ft into society's box and do the things that others around you are doing. I'm trying to tell you not to give in to clout chasing, so you don't have to go down that road because I did make the mistake of trying to fit in.

Where I'm from, my friends were hitting licks, and that's just another word for robbing or breaking into people's houses. They were doing drugs, selling drugs, or scamming. Now, it was easy for me to make the decision not to go into somebody's house because I was too scared to rob anybody. It was also an easy decision not to do drugs because I had some family members whose lives were shattered because of taking drugs.

However, the temptation of selling drugs or scamming was very shiny and possible. In my city, you were taught how to hustle to make it and survive because we all were struggling in our own way. My friends were selling drugs, but they didn't have the same influence and communication skills that I did, so I thought it would be a piece of cake. I soon found out that selling drugs is not how they do it on TV.

I'm a friendly individual who was cool with everybody, and I really wasn't trying to be the tough guy who most people were trying to be when they sold drugs. It was a sunny afternoon, and I had gotten a pack of pills from one of my guys the day before. Although this was my first time trying to sell drugs, it didn't take me long to find a buyer because everybody in my environment knew where the buyers were. Within minutes, one of my friends hit my line and told me that his stepfather wanted to get them.

I was super excited and said to myself, *This is like taking candy from a baby.* Finally, my homeboy and the OG pulled up to my house. OG's are older guys who have lived or were living the street life. I walked out to the car, and I gave him the bag. He gave me his money. I was not really sure what to do next. I just stood there frozen with a smile on my face. OG looked at me, cursed me out, and asked me, "What the Bleep you want now?"

Now, excuse me for a second, but that kind of hurt my feelings. I started thinking to myself, *I can't be a drug dealer if something like this hurt my feelings.* I thought that everybody loves the plug. I thought that it was supposed to be just a small friendly transaction, and we were just supposed to have the best moment or day of our lives. I walked away nervous and offended.

I began to think, *This is not the profession that I want for myself.* The next 2-3 hours were full of deep thought and refection. I began to evaluate my decisions and even the people with whom I was hanging around. I was thinking to myself, *How could I get to this point when I found myself trying to do things that my friends were doing because those things would get me clout*? I was stuck trying to fit into a place that was not made for me.

Listen, clout is not the route! You may be in a space of trying to figure out your life but don't throw it away before it gets started. I'm grateful that I had a bad experience that shifted my mind to rethink my future, but I still didn't accept the signs that the streets weren't for me fully.

I want you not to ignore the signs because there are certain signs that you're going to see that are going to be evident of the roadblocks holding you back from walking in your gift and purpose.

Now, one of the things that was holding me back or was a roadblock to my life was the people who I was around at the time. It didn't really hit me until my best friend was murdered. He was the one good influence who I had who was talking about success. He talked about doing more and being more. When his life was taken, it alarmed me that the streets weren't for me, and I had to figure something else out.

I still remember like it was yesterday when I received the call from his mother. It was early in the morning around 1:00 a.m. or 2:00 a.m. when my phone rang. I picked up the phone, and his mom asked me where a certain set of apartments were because someone told her that her son had been shot. I told her the name of the apartments, and I went back to sleep. Now, anybody who knows me knows that I am a hard sleeper. One minute and 30 seconds later, I realized what his mother said, and I jumped out the bed and grabbed the first set of clothes that I could see.

I jumped into my blue Yukon and sped all the way to the apartments where my best friend was shot. As I arrived at the scene and saw the yellow tape, tears started coming down my face. I was hurt, and I was saying and hoping that it could not be so. I thought, *Maybe there is a mix up, and this is another person.* My boy helped me learn to change my oil, and he showed me how to change a tire. All of those things were flashing back inside my head as I looked at his breathless body on the ground.

Days passed, and it was time for his funeral. As I was sitting down in the church at the funeral, I opened up the obituary, and I saw my face where his face was supposed to be. I slammed it closed and closed my eyes. A few seconds later, I opened it again and I was able to see his face on the obituary. That experience shocked me and scared me like a haunted house on Halloween.

Eventually, I forgot about the obituary experience until three of my other friends passed away that same year. That is crazy, right. I lost 4 friends in one year, and they all died before the age of 22. I had the same experience of seeing my face in their obituaries. I knew then that it was a sign that I had to separate myself from the environment in which I was living. The roadblocks were in front of me, but I kept ignoring the signs of the inevitable.

I had to self-evaluate the fact that I was insane for doing the same thing over and over expecting different results. I spent my time every day playing video games all day or sitting on one of my friend's porch watching the cars drive by, throwing my hands at people I knew, and just talking about nothing.

During those moments, I knew in order to get something different or do something different, I had to be something different. I was ready and committed to doing just that because I was tired of living an average lifestyle, and I was tired of being an average person. Let me ask you something. When was the last time you sat down and self-evaluated the things that are holding you back from being successful?

Take some time to turn of your phone and get alone. Write down a list of the negative things you feel that you need to let go right now. Literally, pause where you are in the book and do this right now because as John Woodson stated, "Without proper self-evaluation, failure is inevitable."

Reflection

When was the last time you completed a self-evaluation?

Write a list of negative things or people you should let go.

Chapter 4
Shift Your Mind

I was looking at this video on Instagram, and I heard coach Kendall Flicklin say, "Your work has to match your want." Now, I knew that I wanted better. I knew that in order to be better, I had to do something different than I had not done before. The only problem was I didn't know where to start. Maybe you're feeling the same way. You're like, *Man, I want to do better and become a better version of myself, but I don't know what to do next.* The first place I suggest you start is your mind. You can't pull from your mind what you do not deposit into it.

I remember getting my first refund check at college and going to the bank to cash it. The teller tricked me into opening a bank account, so I only took out around $400.00. That was enough money for me to go to the mall and get some drip for a local rivalry football game. I went to the mall, and I got a fresh pair of Jordan's, Evisu jeans, a Bulls hat, and a plain tall tee with the sticker on it. Yes, you had to leave the orange sticker on your shirt back then to make a "fashion" statement. Man, that outfit was lit, but those were the only things I remember purchasing from the whole $3,000.00 I received.

About two weeks later, I was getting ready to go on a date with this young lady. I was driving to the ATM to get some to get my money because I didn't really have a debit card. At that time, I only had a savings ATM card to help me get money when I needed it. Guess what? That really didn't help. I pulled up to the ATM, put it in my card, and punched in the amount of money that I needed. I heard this beeping noise, and the screen flashes and told me I had insufficient funds.

Insufficient funds meant that I did not have the amount of money in my bank account that I needed at the time. My heart sank. Sweat started to form on my forehead, and my legs were weakened as I took the walk of shame back to my car.

I learned the hard lesson that I couldn't withdraw something that I didn't deposit inside the bank. See, for many of us, that's what happens to our minds. You know it's time to make the shift, but we haven't deposited something inside our minds intentionally, so when it's time to make a withdrawal, we have insufficient funds.

I did not start being intentional about what I put into my mind until I got introduced into coaching basketball. I went to help with the team and get under a coach's leadership to learn how to be a coach. Knowing how to play the game and coaching the game are totally different. What I didn't know was that the coach would have a life issue that he would have to handle, and that event would shift me from being an assistant coach to the head coach after 2 weeks.

Here I was. I was the head coach at the elementary school that I attended. In an instant, I was called to a higher level as a person. I was responsible for 5th and 6th graders, and I was not even responsible for myself at the moment. I knew I had work that we needed to do to help those young men. I needed to start with their minds, but I had to build my mind and make intentional mental deposits. I knew that growth started with my mind, so I actually picked up a book and started reading it. Yes, I really did. No one told me to read the book. I heard that leaders were readers, so I decided to give it a try.

I was in a form of leadership, and I wanted to be able to read because I would find myself in moments in which I would get frustrated, and I went to what I knew. Where I'm from, all my friends and I cursed when we got angry. However, I was supposed to be leading a group of young men to handle adversity, but I wasn't even built to handle my own adversity at the time.

I didn't have enough in me to pour out to them, so I had to start listening to positive messages and positive music. I had to shift the music I played because I realized that whenever I got angry, I would quote some of the lyrics of the angry music I consumed. This didn't seem bad to me until I had 11-year-olds repeating the words that came from my mouth.

I know what you're thinking, *Here goes another person trying to tell me how to live my life.* The truth is that I'm not trying to tell you how to live your life. I'm just trying to help you avoid some of the things that I experienced. You see, I know that you want to be better, but to get better, growth will be outside your comfort zone.

Let's talk about making a mindset shift and what that process entails. I want to talk about an elevation mindset and a stagnant mindset. A stagnant mindset will say, "I'll stick to what I know. Either I'm good at it, or I'm not." The elevation mindset will say, "I want to learn new things, and I'm fine with taking a risk." A stagnant mindset will say, "It's fine the way it is. There's nothing to change about me." An elevation mindset asks, "Is this really my best? Where can I improve? Where can I get better?" The stagnant mindset would say, "This is a waste of time. There's a lot of things I need to figure out." An elevation mindset will say, "I know this will help me even though this is difficult." The stagnant mindset will say, "It's easier to give up. I'm not really that smart." An elevation mindset will say, "I'll use another strategy. My mistakes will help me learn."

That was just a little short assessment to gauge where you are. Are you thinking, *Coach, I feel like I'm more sort of the stagnant mindset, not flowing and not moving.* Are you thinking, *I have an elevation mindset?* For many of you, whether you're on the left or the right or both, I know you're thinking, *Okay, if I am stagnant, and I want to elevate, what do I do? How do I make the shift?* Now, I'm going to tell you something that's simple, but it's going to be profound. I need you to execute immediately with this one thing that I'm about to say.

Anytime you're faced with a challenge, and you have the opportunity either to take what's comfortable or accept a challenge, accept the challenge. The growth you'll experience inside of the challenge is how you shift from a stagnant mindset to an elevation mindset.

Chapter 5

Shift Your Habits

Now, I'm feeling really good. I've made a shift in my mind. I'm no longer letting negative things or negative people inside my head. I'm protecting my peace as most people say, or I'm protecting my head space. I'm reading more. I'm listening to a lot of different inspirational, motivational things, but I realized that was not enough. I was motivated, but I still wasn't seeing the results I desired.

Let me warn you, motivation is not enough. Your habits are the bridge to your purpose. I went to Atlanta, Georgia, to attend Dr. Eric Thomas's "Average Skill Phenomenal Will" conference. While I was walking inside, they were playing his audio, and the words were, "Stop being average. You're not even good. You were born to be great." At that moment, I knew that I had been born to be great, but the biggest thing I needed to hear was to stop being average.

Not only did I need to stop being average, but I also had to stop my average habits. I was listening to motivational messages. I was reading, but my actions were not changing. I think the thing that convicted me the most was when Dr. Eric Thomas was on the stage. He let us know that he would give us the blueprint, and there would be a lot of people who would walk away and do nothing with it.

Although I wanted to do something in my mind, I hadn't made a change in my habits. Guess what happened? I was that person who went back home on a high feeling of motivation, and I did nothing with the information. Soon, I bought into the method of "Average Skill Phenomenal Will." This means you could have an average skill set, but if you have phenomenal willpower to lock into the habits intentionally, that perspective will get you to your desired level of success. You could surpass those who are so-called better than you, smarter than you, faster than you, or more powerful than you.

You see, I didn't know that just because people were smart or talented, it didn't mean that they weren't going to be successful automatically. I had no clue that they actually put in the work. I also thought that because I was not the smartest or the fastest person, there was no place for me to be successful. I didn't feel like I had the skills or the talent because I didn't have that "it" factor, and nothing stood out about me. However, once I learned that if I had the will to stick to good habits, I would be able to surpass those who were more talented and skilled than me. With this realization, my life began to change at a dramatic speed.

Stop that. I know what you're thinking. You're trying to let some of that stagnant mindset come back into your life. You're trying to let it take over and stop you from thinking that you could surpass those who seemingly are more talented or smarter than you or who feel like they have an upper hand on you. It's the same thing that I thought as well. I'm going to show you some of the habits that helped me that will shift the trajectory of your life.

The first habit is waking up early. This was a challenge for me in the beginning. I was the type of individual who if I had to be at work at seven o'clock, I would get out the bed, brush my teeth, and wash my face at 6:45 a.m. I was a last minute procrastinator. When I heard Dr. Eric Thomas say that he was getting up at 3:00 a.m., I said, "This man must be crazy."

I did hear that success leaves clues, and that was one of the clues that I embraced. Just because your mind says that you want to do something does not mean that your body is going to respect it. This is where your willpower comes into play as it relates to changing your habits. You have to stick to what you said you were going to do intentionally long after the mood in which you said it has changed.

I remember starting to wake up at 6:00 a.m., and I would be sleepy. Then, I mastered getting up at 6:00 a.m., and I tried waking up at 5:30 a.m.. I would wake up and fall asleep again. I was committed to the process of changing my habits, and eventually, I built up the ability to wake up early. I've been waking up at 4:00 a.m. consistently every single morning for the last 4 years.

Now, you must be thinking, *Why am I waking up that early?* Let me tell you. I am waking up early to get a head start. For many of you, you may be like me. You weren't given a network. You weren't given certain opportunities. What you're going to have to do is work harder than everyone else. While most people are waking up at 8:00 a.m., I wake up at 4:00 a.m. Between the hours of 4:00 a.m. and 8:00 a.m., I'm executing and learning the things that it takes to be successful, and I have a four hour jump on those who feel they are successful or better.

You know, one of the biggest things people say is, "I don't have time." Only a small percentage of them are actually busy. However, if you make a commitment to wake up early before everybody else, and you actually are doing some work, this eventually will help you catch those who are in front of you. Let me tell you something. Some people want what it looks like, but they actually don't want to go through what it feels like to achieve their goal.

Setting clear goals was the second habit that I adopted. I used to be the person who had really general goals. I would say things like, "I want to lose 10 pounds." I never said when, how fast, or what I was going to do to get it done. I would say things like, "I want to be better or successful. I want to become wealthy." However, I never included any specific details about how I was going to make those goals happen.

Then, I ran into this acronym that most people may have used in their lives. It's called SMART goals. It stands for specific, measurable, attainable, realistic, and time bound goals. If you type in SMART goals in Google, you'll see plenty of information on SMART goals and ways in which you can implement them. In Chapter 10, I'll give you my T.A.M.E method on how to reach your goals quickly. Until then, look at what SMART goals are and implement them into your life.

The next goal you need to adopt is time blocking. Now, most of us may think, *My life is so busy. I don't have time.* However, that's the problem. That is why you need the time blocked. Time blocking is setting aside a certain amount of time to turn of all of your social media notifications and place your phone on do not disturb.

You shouldn't return text messages during this time. Don't scroll on social media. This is execution time. This time is used specifically to unplug and get away from everybody to complete the task that you need to get done. We're in an age in which people want something right now, and it feels like they have to respond and do things right now. Time blocking helps you do the things that are best for you. That is a habit that is important for you to adopt.

Another habit that you can adopt is listening to something positive everyday. I start my day of every single morning by putting something positive into my mind whether it is a podcast, videos on YouTube, or positive music. I'm always putting something inside myself because I understand that whenever the world wakes up, and the day gets started, they're going to be things that are going to happen that will affect me in a negative way. Adversity is going to come. There's no question about it.

However, my habit of setting my mood by listening to something positive helps when I am hit by life, it doesn't affect me as much. I challenge you to do the same thing. Listen to something positive every single day before you leave your house.

For some of us, we could do it while we're driving in the car, getting ready for work, working out, or showering. Make a commitment to shift your habits, and they will shift your life.

Chapter 6

Shift Your Environment

After you shift your mind and shift your habits, you will make a lot of people uncomfortable. You see, you used to be average. You were doing average things and thinking average thoughts. Now that you have made the shift, you may be a reminder of the average thoughts that they're thinking and the average habits that they have. Sooner or later, you're going to have to shift your environment. Now, these people may not be bad necessarily, but for some of you, they may be.

I remember my first group of friends. I had to separate completely from them because the things that they were doing were bad, and it wasn't a lifestyle that I desired. Remember, I told you I learned really quickly the streets weren't for me, so I had to remove myself from that environment. Your environment is very key when it comes to getting to the next level or getting to your purpose. There will be signs that will let you know that it is time to shift your environment. You'll begin to know when you're talking to those people, and the conversations aren't the same. You will know when they're calling you to go places, and you will say, "You know I don't do that anymore. How is that helping us? Is that making you better?" You'll have those thoughts to yourself, and soon you'll be saying, "I got to get a different circle. I got to get somewhere different. This is not it."

I was thinking the same thing, and I didn't know what to do. I remember being at a meeting for this multi-level marketing company. A multi-level marketing company is what most people call a pyramid scheme. It's when you're working for a company selling a product, and you have to recruit people to sell that product as well. I was sitting in this meeting with this black millionaire, and I was full of excitement. I had seen millionaires before, but I'd never been in the same space or room with a black millionaire. I was thinking to myself, *When it's time for questions and answers, what question can I ask?*

Well, there was a question that was deep down in my soul. At the point where I was in my life, I needed to know the answer. I raised my hand and asked, "What do you do when the people around you don't want greatness at the level that you do?" Well, brace yourself because the answer that he gave me was so simple and profound, but at the time, I didn't think so. He said to me, "Don't limit yourself to the people around you." Now, of course, I said, "Okay, thank you." However, I was thinking to myself, *Where the heck am I going to get around more people? Where the heck am I going to find a new circle?* It's not like people are just putting out ads that said, "Come be my friend."

It wasn't until six months later that this concept made sense to me when I got the opportunity to join Dr. Eric Thomas's personal development group, Breathe University. Dr. Eric Thomas is the number 1 motivational speaker in the world. There were people from all walks of life in one space. They woke up every single day inspired to be great, and the energy was contagious.

You see, I simply learned right there that great environments challenge and inspire you to become better. I was not being challenged to become better, and I was not inspired to reach a new level in my environment.

I'm not telling you that you're going to find people who open their arms to you for free. Sometimes, it may cost you a little money. It was a different thing for me, but I could not afford to miss out on the opportunity to be in this personal development group because I was unwilling to pay $20.00 a month. You see, it wasn't about the money. It was about what I gained on the inside. Being around other people who were more successful than me and were willing to teach me the game was priceless.

Imagine: You shifted your mind. You shifted your habits, and you're now in a space where everybody is thinking the same way as you think. You are in an environment where everybody wants to be great, and they are doing the work daily to make it become a reality. You see, shifting my environment and getting into Breathe University gave me courage. It challenged me to become not only a better person, but also it challenged me to become a better basketball coach. It exposed me to the thought of being an author. In the personal development community, I met 5 other guys who were looking for powerful stories to put inside a book. I quickly said, "Yes," and I started writing my chapter about overcoming being a fatherless child.

Now, that is very funny because you're reading about a person who failed English twice in college. It had nothing to do with me not knowing what I was doing. I allowed the fear of failure to cause me to fail that class. However, being around other authors encouraged me to take a leap of faith to become one as well.

This idea burst in my head that a kid from the south side of Bessemer, Alabama, could be an author. This reality was possible solely because I was in a different environment. I realized I could go and speak to the world because I was exposed to other speakers who were telling their stories and impacting the world.

The thought that I could have my own business and impact others' lives was because I was in an environment of other business owners who told me that it was possible. They also showed me that it was possible.

You see, being in a different environment is important because you will be the top five people with whom you associate. That was one of the principles that my Uncle Herman taught me when I was younger. The principle means you will think and do the same things as the people with whom you surround yourself.

Once I started intentionally lining myself up in an environment where people were trying to chase after greatness and become the best version of themselves, I soon started adopting their habits, learning their secrets, and getting the things that I needed to help me elevate to another level.

Now, let me be real. If you're in a great environment, the people in it are going to hold you accountable. I had to get away from those people who made me feel comfortable and told me what

I wanted to hear. I needed to get in an environment where people would tell me what I needed to hear.

I needed to stop being average. I needed to stop making excuses. I needed to know that growth was outside my comfort zone. I needed to know those things that I wouldn't have known if I wasn't in an environment that challenged me to become better. My new environment held me accountable to do the things that I said I was going to do.

A lot of us may be inspired to say that we want to do things, but when life or adversity hits, we typically fade away from getting those things done.. When you're in a great environment that holds you accountable, the people will not allow you to get beat up by life. They'll help remind you not to make any excuses and never to give up.

When you went through some things, did people give you a pass? Is there anybody around you pushing you not to give up? Are people encouraging you along the way? If the answer to this question is "No," you, my friend, need to hurry and shift your environment.

There are several ways that you can that you can get into a different environment. The first way is to observe the people who are doing good things around you and try to spend time with them. This can be a family member, close friend, or neighbor. I looked up to my uncle when I was growing up. He was the most successful person I knew, but I did not spend time with him to learn from him.

He was busy, so instead of asking him to stop his life to do something with me, I asked him if I could tag along with him. He had a cleaning service, so sometimes, I would go with him and clean, so I could ask him things about business. He would go to the gym at 6:00 a.m. to shoot basketball during the summertime. The ride to the gym and back to his house allowed plenty of time for me to listen to his wisdom.

The next way to get into a different environment is through social media. The game has changed tremendously since I was in my younger years. I was a part of the first wave of social media. We were on platforms called *Black Planet and Bebo. The ability to connect with high level professionals was not as easy as it is today.*

Clubhouse is a new social media platform that allows you instantly to connect with people in different walks of life around the world. This audio based platform is like one big conference call. You have the opportunity to search for rooms that have conversations about topics that interest you. Rooms are basically a closed off space where everybody meets to talk.

There are topics about almost anything. If you want to know about anything, you can just search it. If you can think about it, there is probably a room discussing the topic. People are on the app sharing a wealth of knowledge on topics about which they are passionate. You have the opportunity to be on calls with celebrities to hear directly from them about how they became successful.

The host of the room calls people up to the virtual stage and allows them to ask any question that they would like to ask. You have professionals in different lanes giving away free information that people pay thousands of dollars to get. I have my own club on *Clubhouse* called *When The Ball Goes Flat*. You should download the app and follow the club. We host conversations weekly to support athletes with topics like mental health, financial literacy, and business development. You do have to have an iPhone or iPad to download the app.

You can also join Facebook groups. Facebook groups are places where people meet together who have common interests. You can see inspirational memes or watch live videos of people who are successful. Shifting your environment can change your life for the better and be the boost you need to become the best version of yourself.

Level up your environment today by joining my club on the app Clubhouse.

The Club is called *When The Ball Goes Flat*.

Chapter 7
Find The Gap

Mark Twain said, "The two most important days of your life are the day you were born and the day you find out why." If you didn't know or no one ever told you, you were created for a purpose. You have value inside you, and you are valuable. Now, I can't tell you what your purpose is, and I can't tell you what you're supposed to do with your life, but I can help give you a simple strategy to help you figure it out.

Before I do that, we have to attack your mindset again. I need you to stop thinking that you're not good enough. I'm talking about that thing that you really want to do with your life. I am referring to that thing that is burning inside your soul that is stuck in your mind. Oftentimes, we judge ourselves because we are not perfect, and this is the self-sabotage that keeps us from our purpose.

You don't have to look like them. You don't have to do it like them. You don't have to be as smart as them. You don't have to have millions of social media followers. You just have to be you, and you have to own that. Even better, let me tell you a secret. A lot of times fulfilling your purpose has nothing to do with you. While you're thinking about yourself and your lack of perfection and qualifications, the fastest way to discover your purpose is to find a need and fill it or find your hurt and heal it. Let me run that back for you. The fastest way to find your purpose or to reach the path to your purpose is to find a need and fill it or find your hurt and heal it.

This method is what led me to start coaching high school basketball in 2012. I was at my little brother's basketball game, and they were playing against McAdory High School, home of the great Bo Jackson. I looked and saw that there was only one coach on the bench, and I loved everything that was going on. I loved his system and the way that his guys responded to him. I walked up to him, and I said, "I've been coaching, but I'm looking to get to the next level." I asked if there was a way that I could learn from him. Coach James Poindexter said, "Yes," and my heart was full of joy. There was another coach for the team, but at the time, he had other obligations, so coach Poindexter really needed some help.

Here I was. I was trying to go to the next level of my life, and I had the opportunity to be a high school basketball coach. I saw what looked like a need, and I filled it. While coaching basketball, I learned that there were other needs inside the game itself. I began to help some of my athletes through life issues. Some of them grew up the same way that I did, and they had the same pain points.

They grew up in a single mother household. They dealt with the pain of being a fatherless child. When they experienced those trauma moments, I was able to use my experience and talk them through it. That didn't happen until I actually looked for the need and pursued ways to address it. Coaching basketball helped me see that a lot of athletes needed personal development and skill development outside just the regular practice time. A lot of them didn't have trainers.

I started training athletes because they were getting hurt because they were not getting enough playing time. This realization led to the creation of my brand, Push Elevation. Push Elevation was created in the beginning to fill the need of personal development and training for athletes.

There will be moments that you'll get confirmation or affirmation that lets you know that you're on the right path or doing what you're supposed to do. My confirmation and affirmation occurred when I first started training females. Let me be honest with you, I had a biased opinion about training women athletes, and that was based on my experience at the school where I worked. I did not like the way that they treated their coach, their attitudes, or the way that they were acting. I told myself that I would never train female athletes. Don't be mad at me, ladies. It gets better a little bit later.

After telling myself that I would never train a girl or coach a girl, one of the parents told me that he had a girl who needed some extra work. At that season of life, I was looking to grow as a person, so I said, "Maybe, they're not all the same." I soon found out that the girl with whom I was going to work with had a better work ethic than all the male athletes who were on my team. We met at six o'clock in the morning.

When she arrived, she was happy and listened to everything I said. She did everything I needed. When I first met her, I introduced myself and asked her who she was and how did the team do the following year. She said, "Oh, we did well." Then, I said, "Okay. Well, how did you do?" She was like, "Oh, I sucked." She kind of giggled. I paused because it felt like my blood started to boil inside me. There was work that I needed to do that was more important than basketball, but that was a part of the confirmation that I was getting that I was in the right spot.

I looked at her in her eyes and I told her, "Don't you ever say that in front of me again. As a matter of fact, don't you ever say that again." Subsequently, we began to work on her mind. I began to give her affirmations to speak to herself daily. I began to help her build a prayer time that helped her with her faith as well. After a few weeks of training with me and her sticking to the process, things got good. We knew each other. We were growing, and she was getting better. I was loving it. Then, one day at six o'clock in the morning, we came into the gym, and something seemed a little of, but I didn't think anything about it. I was just thinking to myself, *Maybe she went to a football game the day before, and she's just a little tired.* Now, she knew that I was cool, but one thing I didn't play about was when it was time to grind.

After some time passed, we were stretching and talking, but something was not right. We were getting into the workouts, and she was not going as hard as she normally went. I started asking myself, *What is wrong?* I also thought, *She needs to snap out of it, or I'm just going to end this session and let her go home.* I decided to do methods differently from what I usually did, but I was still trying to process what could be wrong. I wondered if it could have been one of three things. I formed my decision based on the things I saw earlier in our interactions. Number one, I thought maybe she could have got in trouble with her parents and they took her phone or put her on punishment. Number two, I thought maybe it could be a boy. Number three, I thought maybe it could be a boy. After all, in one of the first sessions, a young man came to training with her. After more time passed, I just stopped because I couldn't take it anymore. I said, "What's wrong with you?"

I asked, "It's that boy, isn't it?" She looked at me. She didn't say a word, and she just started crying. My heart started beating so fast, and I started to feel goosebumps inside my body. I thought to myself, *Mike, I told you not to do this. This is it. I told you not to do this.* The truth of the matter is I had no clue of what to do next. Now, in that moment, I just prayed with her because it's all I knew to do. That was the one thing that kind of calmed her down. I think the biggest thing that I learned was building the person was bigger than building the athlete. She felt comfortable enough to open up to me and talk to me because I was willing to find a need to fill it and find a hurt and heal it. That was one of the many moments when I got affirmation that I was in the right line of work of building people and athletes.

On your journey, you'll get signs, but the first thing I need you to do is look around for needs to fall and hurts to heal.

Reflection

Find a need and fill it or find your hurt and heal it.

Chapter 8

What's Your Superpower?

Emma Stone said, "What sets you apart can sometimes feel like a burden, and it's not. And a lot of the time, it's what makes you great. Understanding your strengths and weaknesses help you discover your gifts and know why you're here."

Can I ask you a question? What's your superpower? What's that one thing that you do so well that people often come to you and say, "I wish I can do that," or "I wish I had that ability"? I remember when I was eight years old, I thought I had the real superpower of speed. I would run everywhere. I always would hear my aunt and uncle say, "Stop running. Stop running. Stop running." However, I couldn't stop because I had the gift of speed. I felt like I was faster than time.

One night, I was in Berea, Kentucky with my uncle who raised me. He had his own cleaning service, and he was contracted to clean one of the college buildings at Berea College. That's where he attended college while taking care of me. One night, he was walking to the door to come inside one of the buildings that he was contracted to clean. I was already on the inside with my aunt who was in one of the bathrooms cleaning.

I was eight years old, so I wasn't thinking about the fact that he had a key. Excited to see him, I used my superpower of running to go open the glass door for him. I started running toward the door. It was raining on that day, so it was pretty wet. What I didn't notice was the mat at the door was soaking wet. It was a glass door, so I could see him, and he could see me as I was moving towards the door.

As I was running and doing what I normally did, I felt the hair on my arms raise up because I was going so fast. As I went to hit the door, I slipped headfirst into the glass and busted my head wide open. We had to rush to the emergency room and get stitches because my head was leaking with blood. The only thing that I could think about besides getting scary, six inch needles that the doctor was putting in my head was, *I cannot wait to run again.* It sounds crazy, right? That's how it feels when you know you have a superpower, and you know that you have this gift. No matter what happens, you're in your happy place when you are doing just that.

You're thinking, *I don't have a superpower. There's nothing special about me. I'm different.* Can I tell you something? Embrace your difference. Don't feel bad that you're different from other people because being different is special. I want to challenge you to think about how your difference could be the gateway or the foundation of your superpower.

I remember being in this personal development training. I was learning about the behavioral traits of human beings. I was learning how we're wired and why we do what we do. My coach, Kendall Ficklin, broke it down so simply by using animals.

We all have four animals inside us. As I began to talk about each animal, you'll begin to have thoughts like, *I'm pretty good at that*, or *I don't think that I'm good at that*. After learning about each animal, I'm sure you're going to have an idea of what to explore a little more. You'll learn what possibly could be the superpower you need to impact the world in the manner in which you desire.

We have the lion, the flamingo, the chameleon, and the turtle. We'll start with the lion.

The lion is typically a leader. They like to take charge during a crisis. Lions are not afraid to go first, and they move with a sense of urgency. They want to get things done, and they want things done now. They're not afraid to do the dirty work, and they'll figure out what needs to be done and get it done.

The next animal is the flamingo. They're very sociable individuals. They talk to everybody because they never meet a stranger. They have the ability to inspire others to take action. They're good at thinking quickly on their feet and coming up with things to say or do. They're good at promoting other products, people, or ideas. They are high energy, and they're excited all the time. Have you ever met somebody and you think, *What is he or she always happy about?* There is a high chance that person is a flamingo, and it's a gift to be able to live your life with optimism.

The next animal is a chameleon. Chameleons are great at listening. They're typically called team players. They always put other people's needs before themselves. They're good at recognizing and meeting emotional needs. They're great at adapting and connecting with anybody. Don't ever ask chameleons what they want to eat because they will always say "It doesn't matter. We can eat whatever you want." Chameleons are true servants at heart. They always are leading projects that will help bring change and happiness to a hurting group of people.

The last animal the trainer discussed were turtles. Turtles are usually perfectionists. They're very organized and good at planning. They can see any process through and through. I know what you're thinking, right? Turtles are slow. The typical animal trait that everybody thinks about related to turtles is the fact that they are slow. However, a turtle's superpower is its ability to slow others down to think through things and get them done the right way the first time. Turtles plan and pack for a vacation 3 weeks ahead of time. They also have a plan for the plan after the plan.

I know what you're thinking. You're thinking, *That is me, I'm a little bit of all of those.* You very well may be, but one of the animals stuck out to you the most. Maybe, two of the animals stood out to you very strongly. Maybe, you're that individual or you're that animal all the time.

The way that the animals operate in the training I attended is what I like to call superpowers. The animal or behaviors that we have are very unique. Being organized isn't something that everybody is good at doing. That makes the turtle special and very unique. One may think something so simple isn't special, but that in itself is a superpower that you can use to help you stand out.

What I would suggest you do when it comes to finding out your superpower is ask five of the closest people to you, "What do you think my strength is?" Tell them to name three things that they think are your strengths or three things about which they would come to you for advice or help. After you get a list from those five people, I want you to look at all 15 things. Look for common things repeated on the list. How many times do you see the same gifts that they would come to us for help? Now, I want you to start locking in on those superpowers and embrace them.

I remember I felt that talking too much was a bad thing because I used to get in trouble for it a lot in school. Then, I found out that public speaking is the number one fear in the world. I was thinking to myself, *Why would anybody be afraid of speaking in front of other people?* I had no idea that was one of my superpowers. That was the thing that I didn't feel nervous doing. It felt natural for me to get in front of people and speak. I had no clue that one gift and superpower would be the thing that would help me not only increase my impact, but also they would help me increase my income.

My ability to speak in front of people has led me to be booked to speak all over the United States of America. I've not only locked in on one of my superpowers, but also I also teach athletes how to lock in on their superpowers and get paid for using their gifts.

It's time to stop looking at the things that you are naturally good at doing as something that is normal. View your gifts as superpowers because that's what they are. Take the list you have and run with it as fast as you can.

Just be careful and don't allow your superpower to have you standing with a doctor over your head with a six inch needle.

Chapter 9

Knowing Is Not Enough

Now that you know some of the things that can help you once the ball goes flat, what do you do next? Whether it's shifting your mind, shifting your habits, shifting your environment, filling a need, or even learning what your superpower is, that is not enough. You can pursue your purpose. You could become more than an athlete, but it won't work if you don't put in the effort.

One of the main things I don't want you to do is to become an information junkie. I know you're thinking to yourself, *Well, what is that?* An information junkie is an individual who listens to a lot of things like YouTube videos, podcasts, Clubhouse, Instagram live sessions, but that person doesn't apply any of the information that he or she learns.

I hear the quote, "Knowledge is power," but I disagree. I think applied knowledge is power. It's not enough for you to read this book, put it down, and be the same individual who you are now weeks from now. It's not enough to have a good feeling and to want to change, but you do not take the action steps to change.

You know what you need to do, but if you don't do anything, then nothing will happen.

I heard a quote by Dr. Eric Thomas that said, "Nothing changes if nothing changes." You, my friend, can't make the mistake that I made. I think one of the most frustrating things to experience when you actually start operating in your purpose and finding your superpower is the process of figuring out where to use it. Then, you have to deal with overcoming the feeling of thinking your superpower isn't important enough. There were times when I paid for personal development programs and conferences, and it would take me months to do anything with the information I learned. I would hear the information and know what I needed to do, but I did nothing with it.

My experience reminds me of those programs I attended when I was in elementary school led by people who were doing drugs, but they told us not to do drugs. You should know what you shouldn't do because it's not good for you, but you're still not doing anything with the information that you have. I know you're reading this book, and you're thinking to yourself, *Well, I knew that*. The truth of the matter is that although you know it, you haven't taken the time to implement it and actually stick through it enough to see the results from it.

Have you been an information junkie? Have you just read or heard stuff that sounds good but failed to put it to work to see if it's true or if it would work for you? One of the number one causes for a person becoming an information junkie and remaining an information junkie is being distracted. I'm going to be real with you. There were many reasons for me being distracted, but the main thing for me was playing video games. Now, am I saying something is wrong with playing video games? No, I'm not, but I wanted a successful lifestyle, and I wanted to be great.

The people whose life I wanted to emulate were great, and they weren't playing video games, at least not faithfully like I was every single day. I would sit there and play season after season because, of course, I liked to simulate the season to the All-Star Game on NBA 2K and then simulate the season to the playoffs, so I could win championship after championship. The most hurtful thing was that I wasn't winning any championships with my life.

I was wasting time on social media. I was scrolling for hours and jumping from one social media platform to the next social media platform. Before I knew it, I had no time to do the things I needed to do. I was distracted instead of focusing on my gifts and my superpowers, and I was not filling the need that I needed to fill. I was watching other people live their lives, live their truths, operate in their gifts, fill the apparent needs of others, and heal the hurts that they needed to heal. I was busy watching these things happen and comparing their superpowers to my superpowers, and I didn't apply the information I had learned to be true.

Therefore, you're thinking, *All right, coach, that's me, too. I'm distracted. What do I need to do?* The answer is simple, but I don't know if you're willing to sacrifice to do what it takes to avoid being an information junkie. I completely fasted from all of the things that were distracting me. What does that mean? That means that I stopped playing video games for 60 days. I stopped being on social media for 60 days. I deleted the apps from my phone, so I wouldn't be distracted by other people's lives.

I stopped watching my favorite series on Netflix because I had a problem watching season after season.

Once I did that, I realized I had a lot of time on my hands. The truth of the matter is, it was so boring that I had to execute the things that I wanted to do. I realized I had so many hours to step into the greatness that I wanted for myself and to work on the things that I learned, so I could become the best version of myself. My pursuit of greatness didn't start until I was willing to get rid of the distractions and avoid settling for just knowing information.

I know what you're thinking here. I'm not trying to tell you what to do again, but I am trying to tell you that in order to go up, there are some things you're going to have to give up. Are you willing to sacrifice those things that are distracting you for a short period of time until you gain the discipline to position them in their rightful place in your life? I can't answer that for you, but if you're trying to pursue your purpose and if you're trying to become more than an athlete, this is what it will take.

Chapter 10

T.A.M.E. Your Goals

Benjamin Franklin said, "By failing to prepare, you prepare to fail." Let me tell you something. Preparation is the gateway to elevation. I learned that the hard way, and I don't want you to have to learn it the hard way. I'm not the most organized individual, and preparation was one of the things with which I struggled and didn't value. I told myself the lie that I'm just good under pressure. I felt that last minute things helped me to think better. You know that person who's always late to the barbecue? If dinner is at three o'clock, that person will show up at five or six o'clock. That, my friend, is an individual who has a problem with preparation.

Lets face it, you've spent your entire life living under a schedule that was prepared for you by your parents or even your coaches. Not only did they prepare a schedule for you, but they also followed up to make sure you got the things done that you were supposed to complete. Now, you are responsible for creating your own schedule and following through it to complete your own goals.

I remember being excited because I finally was an adult. I had no clue that adulting would be overrated, and it came with a lot of responsibility. I would hear people talk about goal setting, but I didn't think it was that important. I never made the connection that my lack of goal setting was the cause of me not receiving any results in my life. The question I would dread the most was when someone would ask what my goals were. It was intimidating because I didn't know how to set goals. No one around me taught me how to set goals, so I'm going to show you a simple process that will help you get started today.

For anything that you're going to do, you have to be intentional about it if you're going to make it come to pass. I'm going to do something for you that I don't think anybody did for me. I'm going to give you a strategy to help complete your goals and attack the things you want to get done. Remember, this won't work unless you work it. This is one of my secrets that I use for my clients to help them elevate every area in their lives. This strategy is called the T.A.M.E. method. If you use this method, you will start to see results immediately, but you have to make a commitment and promise to stick with every letter of this method.

I want you to get a notebook and a pen, so you can write this down. Some people use the notes tab on their phone or computer, but I want you to write these things down. Something happens when you put the pen to the paper, and that's what I want you to do. The T in the T.A.M.E. method stands for Target. When you set a goal, I want you to be very specific. Many people are very general when they set goals. I know you've heard people say that they want to lose weight. They almost never lose weight because they were not specified on the amount of weight that they wanted to lose. When you write down your target, make sure it's very specific.

The next letter in the T.A.M.E. method is the A. The A stands for activities. I want you to think about the specific activities you will have to do to complete the targets you have set. For example, I set a target to start being booked as a speaker. The activities that it took to make that happen were getting a speaking coach, learning the business behind speaking, practicing my speeches, and searching for opportunities to speak. Making this list allowed me to remain focused on the things I needed to do in order to reach my target.

The M in T.A.M.E. stands for measurement. You need to have a form of measurement when you are going after your goals to help you measure how well you are progressing towards your goal, how fast you get them done, or how many times you will commit to doing the activities. I remember right after I said I wanted to become a better speaker, one of my former players' college roommate passed away during a road game during basketball season. I knew what it felt like to lose a best friend at such a young age, so I wanted to be there for him the best I could. I decided to record and send him positive videos for 100 straight days. At the end of each week, I would measure how many videos I sent and how many more I had left to go. Measurement keeps you in line and focused on the end goal.

The last letter in the T.A.M.E. method is the E. The E stands for energy. It may seem odd to have energy as a focal point for completing your goals, but it is one of the key components. Most people don't do things when they don't feel like doing them. Let's be honest here, some tasks require more energy than other tasks. By assessing the amount of energy the task will take from you, you know what time of day you need to get the task done.

I run anywhere between 50-70 miles per month. Although I like running, it takes a lot of energy from me. I schedule my running time at 7:00 in the morning because during that time, I am fully energized. I remember when I first started running, I missed my morning run, and I had to do it after work. I learned very fast that after a long day of being physically and mentally drained, I didn't have enough energy to complete my goal with my best effort. Instead of not running at all, I made an adjustment based on my energy.

Mental energy is something that you have to consider while planning your targets as well. People often put off the hard tasks because they are mentally draining. I schedule hard things in the first part of my day because it gives me time to bounce back and replenish the mental drainage. If you try the T.A.M.E. method and commit to doing it for 30 days, you will start to see immediate progress in your life.

Chapter 11

The Power of Serving

I was listening to a podcast one day, and a quote by Zig Ziglar struck my soul. He said, "You can have everything in life you want if you would just help other people get what they want." I bought into this philosophy, and it has been one of the main secrets that helps me do the things that I'm doing today. The lesson I want you to learn in this chapter is if you want to know your purpose or find purpose, you need to serve. Serving is giving up your time and energy intentionally to help someone else.

I believe in eating the food that I cook, so I will never tell you anything that I haven't done myself. One of the main secrets of how I was able to find my purpose and live with my purpose is because I made a decision to serve. Many people don't know that during the 10 years they saw me on the sideline coaching or training with athletes, I was not even paid.

I put in a lot of time and used up a lot of vacation hours at work because I had to leave early to go to basketball games. I spent money and sacrificed time away from my family to serve my way into my purpose. I know what you're thinking. *This may be a challenge for the individuals who only care about themselves and their growth. It may be a challenge for those whose life is only about them.* Well, let me let you in on a secret. The time of my service and sacrifice led me to learning and developing the skills that I needed to become the person I am today.

Every season, I became a better communicator, and I was able to develop the gift of speaking. Every season, I became a better leader because I intentionally was growing to help my staff and athletes become better. I know what you're thinking, *What about me, Coach Mike? How would this have anything to do with my purpose?* Let me give you a secret. Some people might not tell you. People want to help the helpers. If you look around and you're thinking, *Nobody's helping me.* Think about the last person who you helped.

I'm fully aware that you can help people and not receive help. We're not focusing on that. We're focusing on the power of serving. When you're able to do things for other people and become a servant, people notice you without saying a thing. I wasn't trying to be noticed. People just notice those individuals with pure intentions who are looking to help add value to other people.

I remember the first time I got paid for my gift. The money came because I served others. I told you about the development of my gifts. Every time I had to do a pregame speech to my athletes, I was developing the gift. Because of that, I had the opportunity to speak to students in another state. I remember getting called to speak at a youth event in Mississippi.

They asked me how many rooms I needed, and I told them two. The number one person I wanted to join me outside of my wife was my mom. For me, that was super special because I came from a single parent house. My mom was all I had outside of my grandparents and my uncle taking care of me when he did. Being able to bring my mom on the road with me meant a lot.

The event was a two day gig. I spoke to the kids on day one, and I helped with a Spartan race on day 2. After I spoke on the first night, we went back to our hotel to get some rest. I saw someone had given my wife an envelope earlier, so I asked her for it. I opened up the envelope and felt like my heart skipped a beat. My eyes had gotten so wide it felt like they were about to pop out my head. Full of excitement, I threw my check across the room to my wife, so she could see it.

She grabbed the check and looked at it, and she threw it as well. We both were excited because finally, my focus as a servant started to serve me. Look around, there's probably plenty of projects with which you can have an opportunity to serve people and use your superpower.

It may be cutting a neighbor's grass. Learning and doing that could be the start of a lawn care service. It may be babysitting or working for a youth group. That may be the start of your own organization to help the next generation. It may be making food for the homeless. That could be the start of a restaurant. I don't know exactly what you need to do, but I know it starts with serving.

I know earlier we talked about shifting your environment, and there are some environments into which you cannot go unless you have a servant's heart or a service mindset. If you're not going to be the individual who's going to add value to them in that environment, they might not want to give you access. Serving is also a great way to get a mentor. Having a mentor will help shorten your learning curve and help you achieve your goals in life faster. Let me teach you a secret on how you can get a mentor. There is something I am going to forbid you from doing or saying. When you know someone successful from whom you would like to learn, never tell them that you want to "pick their brain." This comes across as offensive to successful people.

They've put in years of hard work, failure, and money into getting where they are, and you think it's ok to just walk up and "pick their brain." That is not ok, but I'm going to teach you an approach that will unlock the answers for you as you pursue your purpose.

If someone has a business or if he or she is doing something that you desire to do, I want you to serve that person three times before you ask for anything. Depending on the relationship, you may get someone who will meet you for lunch and tell you some secret gems, but that person also may hold back. However, if you were to serve this person at least three times, and then say, "Hey, can we go for lunch?", that person may not question your motives and may pour into you because you've served that individual. Mutualism is the door to unlock powerful connections that can help position you for success and the purpose for which you're searching. Mutualism is when two people are equally benefiting each other. Because you have served the individual, he or she has no problem with you benefiting from him or her.

Every skill that I have now, I learned by operating as a servant. I urge you to think about the gifts you have and find somewhere to use them for free. During the process, you'll collect data that will help you become better as well as get closer to pursuing a more fulfilling and purposeful life.

Reflection

Learn to serve three times before asking for anything.

Chapter 12

Patiently Aggressive

Listen, I cannot let you go without helping you understand what it's going to take to walk into your purpose after you're done with sports. Understand this, you are more than an athlete. Elevation will be hard, but it's very possible.

One of the things about purpose that I want you to understand is it's something that you have to pursue. You have to go after it as hard as you did when you were chasing rings while playing the sport that you love. I want you to become patiently aggressive. I want you to know that it takes time but work like there's no time.

During the time that I'm writing this book, we're going through a pandemic, and we have experienced a lot with COVID-19. The biggest thing is no matter how young you are, the virus is taking people out in 14 days, and you have no clue how much time you have. Now, I'm not saying that to scare you or put any fear inside you. I just want you to know that you can't waste any time when it comes to locking into your purpose and living a purposeful life after sports. You will have to have a work ethic. As I said before in previous chapters, it won't work unless you do.

I do want you to understand that you need to stick with the process of growth. There are going to be high highs, and there are going to be low lows. I've been helping athletes transition from sports for years now. I was working with one of my clients, and he wanted to become a speaker and go inside the schools and impact lives with his lessons the same way that I do. Waking up early was one of the missions that I gave him in order to prepare his content and do the things that he had to do. I told him, "We have to wake up for 30 days straight between 4:00 a.m. and 6:00 a.m. to get the things done that we need to get to the next level."

After day 10, I asked him how things were going. He said that he may need to focus on staying up late because waking up early wasn't working. I suggested that he go to bed earlier to help him successfully wake up on time. He did what most people do when things get hard. He found a reason not to follow through. I told him, "You haven't given it enough time yet. You had your same habits for 21 years. They're not going to go away after 10 days."

I know you've heard the words, "trust the process", and it may seem cliché, but it's just that simple. The same way that it took you to develop and learn to play as an athlete will be the same process that it takes when pursuing your purpose. You worked at that every single day. You had practice every single day. You also may have gotten individual training. Whenever you weren't doing it, you were thinking about it.

This is the same aggression that you have to have towards your purpose. You need the same patience and understand that you're just growing through some things. Life will hit you with adversity, but I want you to understand that your purpose is on the other side of adversity. Be patient while going through and growing through the things that life throws at you.

Life is going to test you to see how badly you want it. I want you to understand that you can have, be, and do whatever you want to do as long as you're willing to go through and grow through what it takes to get there. One of the biggest things to help you understand what it means to be patiently aggressive is to understand that you have to give yourself grace along this transition. You also need to have a mamba mentality to attack the things that you want in life. It may sound a little confusing, but it's just as simple as it can be.

I remember my journey of building my own personal brand. It was rough, and it was tough, and some days, it's still hard. Nobody knew who I was. Nobody wanted to watch my videos. Nobody wanted to buy my products. Nobody wanted to bring me in to speak. However, it was simple. I was just growing through the process of building myself and growing into who I was called to be.

Was it hard? Yes. Was it frustrating? Yes. However, I still made a commitment to show up every single day. Let me ask you something. What would your life look like if you made a commitment to show up every single day and do one thing aggressively until you see it all the way through? What would your life look like if you put all your energy and effort from the pit of your stomach deep down in your soul and attacked it the same way that you attacked any of your opponents when you were playing the game?

I know you'll live a happy, purposeful, and fulfilling life by understanding that you have to work for it and be aggressive, but at the same time, be patient and know that pain and setback are parts of the process. It's going to be the recipe that you need to not only step into your purpose but also to enjoy the journey of growing.

Do something for me. Look at your calendar inside your phone. What does it look like? If it's very blank and there's no plan, then you're probably not being aggressive. When I got to the point at which my schedule had something towards my purpose, my gifts, and my dreams every single day, that's when I started seeing momentum. That's when I started seeing things happen for me.

Opportunity comes with activity, and I know you want an opportunity to walk into your gift and walk into your purpose. However, that won't happen if you don't have a work ethic. While having a work ethic and putting in work are the keys to unlocking your greatness, I know that we're living in a microwave society, and everybody wants it right now. I'm going to challenge you to be patient and be faithful along your journey because it may not come right now, but if you chop a tree in the same spot long enough, eventually, it'll fall down.

If you Google any of the people who society deems to be successful, I guarantee you that it took them years to get there. I also guarantee that it took them going through plenty of adversity and failure to reach the level of success where they are now. The life that you have ahead of you is more important and more purposeful than the life that you have behind you.

You are more than an athlete. If you put in the work and serve others, you're bound to find your purpose.

When The Ball Goes Flat 6 Week Boot Camp

Sign up today at
www.michaelbarhamelevates.com

Epilogue

Now that you have reached the end of this book, you have the information you need to pursue your purpose after sports. You have the opportunity to shift your thinking, understand your value, and use your gift to impact the world.

Don't just read this book and become an information junkie. Put it into action. Elevate and become more than an athlete.

The following is a summary of the concepts that have been discussed in this book to help you become the best version of yourself and start pursuing your purpose.

Chapter 1: Understand that you are not alone in the process. There are millions of athletes who have expressed the pain of sports ending. Now, it's time to build up the person instead of the athlete.

Chapter 2: Embrace the responsibility for your growth and commit to controlling what you can control.

Chapter 3: Self-evaluate to get a clear understanding of what's in between who you are and the elevation you desire.

Chapter 4: Learn the importance of how and why you have to shift your thinking from a stagnant mindset to an elevated mindset.

Chapter 5: Learn the power of having good habits and identify the habits you should start adding to your life right away.

Chapter 6: Understand how changing your environment can set you up for the success you desire.

Chapter 7: Know that you are valuable and share your value with the world.

Chapter 8: Discover your unique superpower and learn how being different isn't a bad thing.

Chapter 9: Go to work ASAP and avoid being ok with just having the knowledge of what successful people do.

Chapter 10: Learn the T.A.M.E. method to help you prepare and attack the goals you set for yourself.

Chapter 11: Serve others and use the act of serving others to help you find your purpose.

Chapter 12: Understand that the transition will be hard, so you have to give yourself grace along the process. Recognize that your work ethic is vital to pursuing your purpose.

About the Author

Michael Barham was born and raised in Bessemer, AL. He is a husband to his wonderful wife, Kaitlyn, and he is a father to his two beautiful daughters, Khloe and Kylie. His coaching journey started when he accidentally became a little league basketball head coach in 2010. Later, he had the opportunity to coach high school basketball as an assistant coach. Upon seeking to become a better coach for his players, Michael sought after personal and professional development. The tools he learned from Dr. Eric Thomas and Kendall Ficklin inspired him to create his personal brand, Push Elevation.

Since creating Push Elevation, Michael has had the opportunity to help increase the performance of individuals and organizations in the areas of communication, team building, and leadership. His focus shifted after witnessing his former players experience tough transitions in life after sports. He knew he had to develop a way to fill the need and support athletes after sports. He created programs to help athletes pursue their purpose and build their own brands. His first book, *Purpose Pioneers* became an Amazon Bestseller. Michael has been featured in the popular blog, Voyage ATL, for his dedication to be a trailblazer for his community.

Michael has over 5 years of experience as a business coach and consultant. As a DISC expert and a professional speaker, he has trained thousands of students to unlock their potential and perform at a high level.

www.ingramcontent.com/pod-product-compliance
Lightning Source LLC
Chambersburg PA
CBHW070949180426
43194CB00041B/1996